I0845758

The Story of Elie Wiesel

In the small town of Sighet, nestled in the picturesque Carpathian Mountains of present-day Romania, Elie Wiesel was born on September 30, 1928. He was born into a devout Jewish family, and his early life was shaped by the rich traditions and customs of his faith.

Elie grew up in a tight-knit community where Jewish customs and rituals were an integral part of daily life. He was raised in a home where the flame of Jewish faith burned bright, with his father, Shlomo Wiesel, serving as a respected leader in the local Jewish community. From a young age, Elie was immersed in the teachings of the Torah and the history of the Jewish people, instilling in him a deep sense of identity and pride in his heritage.

Despite the economic challenges faced by many in Sighet, Elie's childhood was filled with moments of joy and laughter. He had a close relationship with his three sisters, Hilda, Bea, and Tzipora, and their family bond was strengthened by their shared faith and the warmth of their familial love. Elie was known for his insatiable curiosity and thirst for knowledge, often engaging in spirited discussions with his father and other members of the community about the mysteries of the universe and the complexities of human nature.

As Elie grew older, the dark clouds of World War II began to cast their shadow over Sighet. Anti-Semitic sentiment and discrimination against Jews were on the rise, and the once idyllic town was soon enveloped by an atmosphere of fear and uncertainty. Elie's world was shattered when, in 1940, Sighet was annexed by Hungary, and his family was subjected to increasingly harsh restrictions and persecution.

Despite the growing danger, Elie's faith remained a source of strength and solace. He sought comfort in the teachings of the Kabbalah, a mystical branch of Jewish philosophy, and found solace in the rituals and prayers that had been passed down through generations. However, the escalating threats against the Jewish community in Sighet would soon test Elie's faith in ways he could never have imagined.

The peaceful existence Elie had known in Sighet was shattered in 1944, when the Nazis invaded Hungary and began implementing their genocidal plan to annihilate the Jewish population. Elie and his family were forcibly deported to Auschwitz, the notorious concentration camp in Poland, where they were separated upon arrival. Elie's mother and youngest sister, Tzipora, were tragically killed in the gas chambers, while Elie and his father were sent to work as slave laborers, enduring unspeakable horrors and witnessing the depths of human depravity.

The trauma of his childhood experiences in Sighet, the loss of loved ones, and the atrocities he witnessed during the Holocaust would leave an indelible mark on Elie, shaping his worldview and inspiring his lifelong commitment to bearing witness and fighting against injustice. His childhood in Sighet, with its rich traditions and profound challenges, would serve as a crucible that would shape the course of his life and set him on a path to becoming a towering figure in the fight for human rights and social justice.

Post-War Years and Beginnings as a Writer

After surviving the unspeakable horrors of the Holocaust, Elie Wiesel found himself grappling with the weight of his traumatic experiences as he embarked on the next chapter of his life. Rescued from Buchenwald by Allied forces, he was faced with the daunting task of rebuilding his shattered world. It was during this tumultuous period that Elie discovered the redemptive power of the written word.

Despite the immense challenges he faced, Elie was determined to give voice to the atrocities he had witnessed. He found solace in putting pen to paper, as he poured out his memories and emotions onto the page. Writing became a cathartic outlet for Elie, a way to make sense of the senseless, and a means to preserve the memory of those who perished in the Holocaust.

In 1955, Elie's seminal work, "Night," was published, marking the beginning of his literary career. This powerful memoir, which recounted his harrowing experiences during the Holocaust, was met with critical acclaim and established Elie as a prominent voice in Holocaust literature. Through haunting prose, Elie vividly described the horrors of the concentration camps, the loss of his family, and the profound impact the Holocaust had on his faith and identity.

"Night" was just the beginning of Elie's prolific literary output. He went on to write numerous memoirs, novels, essays, and speeches, all bearing witness to the indescribable suffering and unfathomable resilience of the human spirit. His works delved into the complexities of memory, trauma, and the moral responsibility to remember and learn from the past.

Elie's writing resonated with readers around the world, as he eloquently conveyed the unfathomable horrors of the Holocaust and the universal themes of human suffering, resilience, and the search for meaning in the face of adversity. His powerful words served as a call to action, urging readers to confront the darkness of the past and strive for a more just and compassionate future.

Humanitarian Work and Global Impact

As Elie Wiesel's literary career flourished, he channeled his unwavering commitment to social justice into impactful humanitarian work. Drawing on his own experiences as a Holocaust survivor, Elie became a tireless advocate for human rights, working tirelessly to prevent genocide, promote tolerance, and combat injustice on a global scale.

With his words as his weapon, Elie traveled the world, speaking passionately about the dangers of hatred, prejudice, and indifference. He delivered powerful speeches at international forums, universities, and conferences, captivating audiences with his poignant messages of remembrance, compassion, and hope.

Elie's advocacy extended beyond his speeches and writings. He played a crucial role in the establishment of the United States Holocaust Memorial Museum in Washington, D.C., serving as Chairman of the Presidential Commission on the Holocaust. His efforts helped ensure that the Holocaust would not be forgotten, and that its lessons would be preserved for future generations.

In addition to his work on Holocaust remembrance, Elie was a vocal advocate for other marginalized groups. He lent his voice to campaigns against apartheid in South Africa, oppression in the Soviet Union, and genocide in places like Cambodia and Bosnia. He used his influence to speak up for the voiceless, challenging oppressive regimes and shining a light on human rights abuses around the world.

Elie's humanitarian work earned him numerous accolades, including the Nobel Peace Prize in 1986. This prestigious honor recognized his extraordinary efforts to promote peace, justice, and understanding in a world still plagued by violence and intolerance. Elie used the global platform provided by the Nobel Prize to further amplify his messages of remembrance, compassion, and social responsibility.

Despite facing criticism and controversy for his outspoken advocacy, Elie remained resolute in his commitment to fight for those who could not fight for themselves. He believed that silence in the face of injustice was not an option, and that each individual had a moral obligation to stand up for what is right.

Academic Career and Literary Contributions

After surviving the horrors of the Holocaust, Elie Wiesel's unwavering commitment to remembering the past and bearing witness to the atrocities he had experienced took shape in his academic pursuits and literary contributions. As a scholar and writer, Wiesel left an indelible mark on the fields of Holocaust studies, Jewish literature, and human rights discourse, with his extensive body of work beyond his seminal memoir, "Night."

Following his liberation from the concentration camps, Wiesel embarked on a journey of intellectual exploration, seeking to make sense of the unfathomable brutality he had witnessed. He pursued his studies with a fervent determination, obtaining degrees in literature, philosophy, and theology from the Sorbonne in Paris and later earning a Ph.D. in philosophy from Boston University.

In 1972, Wiesel joined the faculty of Boston University as a professor of humanities, where he would go on to make a profound impact on generations of students. His passionate teaching style and thought-provoking lectures on ethics, theology, and Jewish philosophy captivated his students and colleagues alike, earning him a reputation as a beloved and inspiring professor.

As a scholar, Wiesel delved into the depths of human morality and spirituality, grappling with questions of faith, memory, and the human condition. He authored numerous scholarly articles and delivered countless lectures on topics ranging from the ethics of memory to the theological implications of the Holocaust. Wiesel's scholarly work was characterized by his deep introspection, meticulous research, and unwavering commitment to truth and justice.

However, it was Wiesel's literary contributions that would earn him worldwide acclaim and solidify his place as a towering figure in the world of letters. Beyond "Night," his haunting memoir that chronicled his experiences during the Holocaust, Wiesel wrote extensively in various genres, including memoirs, novels, essays, and speeches.

His memoirs, such as "Dawn" and "Day," provided searing accounts of his post-Holocaust journey, grappling with survivor guilt, and the challenges of rebuilding a shattered life. In his novels, such as "The Town Beyond the Wall" and "The Gates of the Forest," Wiesel explored themes of identity, memory, and faith, drawing from his own experiences and weaving them into powerful narratives that resonated with readers around the world.

Wiesel's essays and speeches were equally powerful, addressing pressing social and political issues, advocating for human rights, and challenging the status quo. He was known for his eloquent and poignant prose, his ability to convey the depths of human suffering and resilience, and his unwavering commitment to confronting injustice and promoting compassion and understanding among all people.

Personal Life

Beyond the towering figure of Elie Wiesel as a Holocaust survivor, writer, and scholar, lay a deeply personal side that was marked by profound relationships and cherished familial bonds. Wiesel's personal life was a tapestry of love, loss, and enduring connections, shaping him into the man he was beyond his public persona.

Wiesel's journey into love and marriage began in 1969 when he met Marion Erster Rose, a Holocaust survivor herself. The two kindred spirits, united by their shared past, formed a deep bond, and in 1969, they tied the knot, embarking on a lifelong partnership that would endure through the trials and tribulations of life.

As a husband, Wiesel was known for his unwavering devotion and tenderness towards Marion. Despite the challenges that life threw at them, including the pain of their shared past and the demands of Wiesel's career as a writer and activist, their bond remained steadfast. Marion was a pillar of support for Wiesel, providing him with comfort, solace, and love in the face of life's adversities.

Wiesel's role as a father was equally significant in his personal life. He and Marion were blessed with a son, Elisha Wiesel, who would become a cherished source of joy and pride for the couple. Wiesel's love for his son was unconditional, and he took great care to instill in Elisha the values of compassion, tolerance, and the importance of standing up for justice and human rights.

Legacy and Impact

Elie's contributions to society were widely recognized during his lifetime, including being awarded the Nobel Peace Prize in 1986, the Presidential Medal of Freedom in 1992, and the Congressional Gold Medal in 1985, among many others. These honors serve as a testament to Elie's unwavering commitment to promoting peace, tolerance, and understanding among all people.

Even after his passing in 2016, Elie's legacy continues to inspire and influence future generations. His words and actions remain a beacon of hope in a world still plagued by intolerance and injustice. His message of remembrance, compassion, and social responsibility continue to resonate, urging individuals and communities to strive for a better, more just world.

Elie Wiesel was known for his eloquent and poignant words, both written and spoken. As a Holocaust survivor, writer, and activist, Wiesel's words encapsulate his deep wisdom, profound insights, and unwavering commitment to advocating for human rights, remembering the Holocaust, and promoting peace and justice in the world. From his seminal work "Night" to his countless speeches, interviews, and essays, Wiesel's words continue to inspire, educate, and provoke reflection, serving as a testament to his enduring legacy as a thought leader and voice for the voiceless. We will explore some of Elie Wiesel's most powerful and thought-provoking quotations, which continue to resonate with relevance and significance in our modern times.

In the word question, there is a beautiful word - quest. I love that word. We are all partners in a quest. The essential questions have no answers. You are my question, and I am yours - and then there is dialogue. The moment we have answers, there is no dialogue. Questions unite people.

If life is not a celebration, why remember it ? If life --- mine or that of my fellow man --- is not an offering to the other, what are we doing on this earth?

Writing is not like
painting where you
add. It is not what
you put on the canvas
that the reader sees.
Writing is more like
a sculpture where you
remove, you eliminate
in order to make the
work visible. Even
those pages you
remove somehow
remain.

Man, as long as he
lives, is immortal.
One minute before
his death he shall
be immortal. But
one minute later,
God wins.

A religious person
answers to God, not
to the elected or
non-elected
official.

I did not deny
God's existence,
but I doubted his
absolute justice.

An immoral society betrays
humanity because it
betrays the basis for
humanity, which is memory.
An immoral society deals
with memory as some
politicians deal with
politics. A moral society
is committed to memory:
I believe in memory. The
Greek word alethia means
Truth, Things that cannot
be forgotten. I believe in
those things that cannot be
forgotten and because of
that so much in my work
deals with memory... What
do all my books have in
common? A commitment to
memory.

Night is purer than
day; it is better for
thinking and loving
and dreaming.
At night everything
is more intense, more
true. The echo of
words that have been
spoken during the day
takes on a new and
deeper meaning.

Yet another last night. The last night at home, the last night in the ghetto, the last night in the train, and, now, the last night in Buna. How much longer were our lives to be dragged out from one 'last night' to another?

Mankind must
remember that peace
is not God's gift to
his creatures; peace
is our gift to each
other.

With every cell of my being and with every fiber of my memory I oppose the death penalty in all forms. I do not believe any civilized society should be at the service of death. I don't think it's human to become an agent of the angel of death.

For the dead and the
living, we must bear
witness. Not only are
we responsible for the
memories of the dead,
we are responsible for
what we do with those
memories.

Drawn to childhood,
the old man will seek
it in a thousand
different ways.

My faith is a wounded
faith, but my life is
not without faith.
I didn't divorce God,
but I'm quarrelling
and arguing and
questioning, it's a
wounded faith.

Perhaps some day
someone will explain
how, on the level of
man, Auschwitz was
possible; but on the
level of God, it will
forever remain the
most disturbing of
mysteries.

The silence of
two people is
deeper than the
silence of one.

Only the guilty are
guilty: the children
of killers are not
killers, but
children.

I write to understand
as much as to be
understood.

One more stab to
the heart, one more
reason to hate. One
less reason to live.

Sometimes we must interfere. When human lives are endangered, when human dignity is in jeopardy, national borders and sensitivities become irrelevant. Whenever men or women are persecuted because of their race, religion, or political views, that place must - at that moment - become the center of the universe.

To forget the dead
would be akin to
killing them a
second time.

But where was I to start?
The world is so vast,
I shall start with the
country I knew best,
my own. But my country
is so very large. I had
better start with my
town. But my town, too,
is large. I had best
start with my street. No,
my home. No, my family.
Never mind, I shall
start with myself.

If you ask me what I
want to achieve, it's to
create an awareness,
which is already the
beginning of teaching.

All collective
judgments are wrong.
Only racists make
them. No human race
is superior; no
religious faith is
inferior.

Philosophy is a slow
process of logic and
logical discourse: A
bringing B bringing C
and so forth. In
mysticism you can
jump from A to Z. But
the ultimate objective
is the same.
It's knowledge.
It's truth.

Whenever an angel
says "Be not afraid!"
you'd better start
worrying. A big
assignment is on
the way.

Hunger is isolating;
it may not and cannot
be experienced
vicariously. He who
never felt hunger can
never know its real
effects, both tangible
and intangible. Hunger
defies imagination;
it even defies memory.
Hunger is felt only in
the present.

When a person
doesn't have
gratitude,
something is
missing in his
or her humanity.
A person can almost
be defined by his or
her attitude toward
gratitude.

Man's strength
resides in his
capacity and desire
to elevate himself, so
as to attain the good.
To travel step by step
toward the heights.
And that is all he can
do. To reach heaven
and remain there is
beyond his powers:
Even Moses had to
return to earth. Is it
the same for evil?

How are we to reconcile our supreme duty towards memory with the need to forget that is essential to life? No generation has had to confront this paradox with such urgency. The survivors wanted to communicate everything to the living: the victim's solitude and sorrow, the tears of mothers driven to madness, the prayers of the doomed beneath a fiery sky.

You're at the bottom
of the mountain. May
you climb up without
suffering.

... you do not
leave a library;
if you do what it
wants you to do,
you are taking it
with you.

Man asks and God
replies but we don't
understand his
replies because they
dwell in the depths of
our souls and remain
there until we die.

At Auschwitz, not only
man died, but also the
idea of man. To live in
a world where there is
nothing anymore,
where the executioner
acts as god, as judge—
many wanted no part of
it. It was its own heart
the world incinerated
at Auschwitz.

I feel that books, just
like people, have a
destiny. Some invite
sorrow, others joy,
some both.

For me, every hour
is grace. And I feel
gratitude in my
heart each time I
can meet someone
and look at his or
her smile.

How can one explain
the attraction terror
holds for some minds
— and why for
intellectuals? . . .
In a totalitarian and
terrorist regime, man
is no longer a unique
being with infinite
possibilities and
limitless choices but
a number, a puppet...

When you die and go to heaven our maker is not going to ask, 'why didn't you discover the cure for such and such? why didn't you become the Messiah?' The only question we will be asked in that precious moment is 'why didn't you become you?'

Every single human
being is a unique
human being. And,
therefore, it's so
criminal to do
something to that
human being,
because he or she
represents
humanity.

Better that one heart
be broken a thousand
times in the retelling,
he has decided, if it
means that a thousand
other hearts need not
be broken at all.

We must choose
between the violence
of adults and the
smiles of children.
Between the ugliness
of hate and the will
to oppose it. Between
inflicting suffering
and humiliation on
our fellow man and
offering him the
solidarity and hope
he deserves.

There is a difference
between a book of two
hundred pages from the
very beginning, and a
book of two hundred
pages which is the
result of an original
eight hundred pages.
The six hundred are
there. Only you don't
see them.

There are victories of
the soul and spirit.
Sometimes, even if you
lose, you win.

Why is war such an
easy option? Why does
peace remain such an
elusive goal? We know
statesmen skilled at
waging war, but where
are those dedicated
enough to humanity
to find a way to
avoid war.

The more you ask
certain questions,
the more dangerous
they become.

No one is as capable of gratitude as one who has emerged from the kingdom of night. We know that every moment is a moment of grace, every hour an offering; not to share them would mean to betray them. Our lives no longer belong to us alone; they belong to all those who need us desperately.

Life is really
fascinated only by
death. It vibrates
only when it comes in
contact with death.

Since God is, He is
to be found in the
questions as well
as the answers.

[Memory] is a passion
no less powerful or
pervasive than love.
It is [the ability] to
live in more than one
world, to prevent the
past from fading,
and to call upon
the future to
illuminate it.

When adults wage war,
children perish.

I came to the
conclusion that I
am free to choose my
own suffering.
But I am not free to
consent to someone
else's suffering.

I still believe in man in spite of man. I believe in language even though it has been wounded, deformed, and perverted by the enemies of mankind. And I continue to cling to words because it is up to us to transform them into instruments of comprehension rather than contempt. It is up to us to choose whether we wish to use them to curse or to heal, to wound or to console.

We believed in God,
trusted in man, and
lived with the
illusion that every
one of us has been
entrusted with a
sacred spark.

... True, we are often too weak to stop injustices; but the least we can do is to protest against them. True, we are too poor to eliminate hunger; but in feeding one child, we protest against hunger. True, we are too timid and powerless to take on all the guards of all the political prisons in the world; but in offering our solidarity to one prisoner we denounce all the tormentors. True, we are powerless against death; but as long as we help one man, one woman, one child live one hour longer in safety and dignity, we affirm man's [woman's] right to live.

The philosophers
are wrong: it is not
words that kill,
it is silence.

You know, words have
strange destiny, too.
They grow. They get
old. They die. They
come back.

I swore never to be
silent whenever and
wherever human beings
endure suffering and
humiliation. We must
always take sides.
Neutrality helps the
oppressor, never the
victim. Silence
encourages the
tormentor, never
the tormented.

Human suffering
anywhere concerns
men and women
everywhere.

Words can be turned
into spears. They
can be turned into
prayers. It's a
strange world that
you are in. But you
deal with words.

Even in darkness it
is possible to create
light and encourage
compassion. That it
is possible to feel
free inside a prison.
That even in exile,
friendship exists
and can become an
anchor. That one
instant before
dying, man is still
immortal.

You shouldn't act
as a spokesperson
for someone who's
trying to impose
his will on you.

No human being is illegal. That is a contradiction in terms. Human beings can be beautiful or more beautiful, they can be fat or skinny, they can be right or wrong, but illegal? How can a human being be illegal?

From time immemorial, people have talked about peace without achieving it. Do we simply lack enough experience? Though we talk peace, we wage war. Sometimes we even wage war in the name of peace..... War may be too much a part of history to be eliminated—ever.

Friendship marks a
life even more deeply
than love. Love risks
degenerating into
obsession, friendship
is never anything
but sharing.

We tried. It was not easy. At first, because of the language; language failed us. We would have to invent a new vocabulary, for our own words were inadequate, anemic. And then too, the people around us refused to listen; and even those who listened refused to believe; and even those who believed could not comprehend. Of course they could not. Nobody could. The experience of the camps defies comprehension.

Emphasis must be put
on learning: there is
no substitute to
education. It can be
briefly formulated in
a few words: always,
whatever you do in
life, think higher
and feel deeper.

The opposite of love
is not hate, it's
indifference. The
opposite of art is
not ugliness, it's
indifference. The
opposite of faith
is not heresy, it's
indifference. And the
opposite of life is
not death, it's
indifference.

I am myself only when
I work. I work for
four hours without
interruption. Then I
stop for my studies.
But these four hours
are really mine.

We're alone, but
we are capable of
communicating to
one another both
our loneliness and
our desire to break
through it. You say,
'I'm alone.' Someone
answers, 'I'm alone
too.' There's a shift
in the scale of
power. A bridge is
thrown between the
two abysses.

Some writings could
sometimes, in moments
of grace, attain the
quality of deeds.

It seemed as impossible to conceive of Auschwitz with God as to conceive of Auschwitz without God. Therefore, everything had to be reassessed because everything had changed. With one stroke, mankind's achievements seemed to have been erased. Was Auschwitz a consequence or an aberration of "civilization"? All we know is that Auschwitz called that civilization into question as it called into question everything that had preceded Auschwitz. Scientific abstraction, social and economic contention, nationalism, xenophobia, religious fanaticism, racism, mass hysteria. All found their ultimate expression in Auschwitz.

Once you bring life into the world, you must protect it. We must protect it by changing the world.

I pray to the God
within me that He
will give me the
strength to ask Him
the right questions.

I was the accuser, God
the accused. My eyes
were open and I was
alone—terribly
alone in a world
without God and
without man.

What is good for me is
not necessarily good
for someone else.
Writing is so personal,
so profoundly and
terribly personal. Your
entire personality goes
into every word. The
hesitation between one
word and another is
filled with many
centuries,
much space.

Certain things,
certain events, seem
inexplicable only
for a time: up to the
moment when the veil
is torn aside.

I have not lost
faith in God. I
have moments of
anger and protest.
Sometimes I've been
closer to him for
that reason.

Young people want to
learn, they are thirsty
for knowledge, they
want to understand and
remember. The main
thing is to teach them
where not to go.
Oppression, not to go;
dictatorship, not to go;
racism and prejudice,
absolutely not to go.
This is a moral plan
[for society].

Just as man cannot
live without dreams,
he cannot live
without hope. If
dreams reflect the
past, hope summons
the future.

War is like night,
she said. It covers
everything.

The darkest days in my life after the war, after the war, was when I discovered that the ... most of the members and commanders of the Einsatz group that were doing the killings, not even in gas chambers, but killing with machine guns, had college degrees from German universities and PhD's and MD's. Couldn't believe it.

There is much to be done,
there is much that can be
done... One person of
integrity, can make a
difference, a difference of
life and death. As long as one
dissident is in prison, our
freedom will not be true. As
long as one child is hungry,
our lives will be filled with
anguish and shame. What all
these victims need above all
is to know that they are not
alone; that we are not
forgetting them, that when
their voices are stifled we
shall lend them ours, that
while their freedom depends
on ours, the quality of our
freedom depends on theirs.

Because I remember,
I despair. Because I
remember, I have the
duty to reject
despair.

Most people think
that shadows follow,
precede or surround
beings or objects. The
truth is that they
also surround words,
ideas, desires, deeds,
impulses and
memories.

Life is not a fist.
Life is an open
hand waiting for
some other hand
to enter it.

I needed to know
that there was such
a thing as love and
that it brought
smiles and joy in
its wake.

It was pitch dark. I could hear only the violin, and it was as though Juliek's soul were the bow. He was playing his life. The whole of his life was gliding on the strings—his last hopes, his charred past, his extinguished future. He played as he would never play again...When I awoke, in the daylight, I could see Juliek, opposite me, slumped over, dead. Near him lay his violin, smashed, trampled, a strange overwhelming little corpse.

In the face of suffering, one has no right to turn away, not to see. In the face of injustice, one may not look the other way. When someone suffers, and it is not you, that person comes first. One's very suffering gives one priority... To watch over one who grieves is a more urgent duty than to think of God.

Only fanatics — in religion as well as in politics — can find a meaning in someone else's death.

I think this century
more than any other
really has seen the
phenomenon of people
being uprooted in such
numbers, such a degree.
They even have a word
for it: The refugees.
It's a new word, a 20th
Century word, but
refugee is actually a
misnomer...Once upon a
time refugee meant
somebody who has a
refuge, found a place, a
haven where he could
find refuge.

None of us is
in a position to
eliminate war, but
it is our obligation
to denounce it and
expose it in all its
hideousness. War
leaves no victors,
only victims.

[Friedrich]
Nietzsche said
something
marvellous, he
said "Madness is
not a consequence
of uncertainty but
of certainty", and
this is fanaticism.

To remain silent and
indifferent is the
greatest sin of all.

Always remember, my good friends, that there is one sin we must never commit and it is to humiliate another person or to allow another person to be humiliated in our presence without us screaming and shouting and protesting.

I have no doubt that
faith is only pure when
it does not negate the
faith of another. I have
no doubt that evil can
be fought and that
indifference is no
option. I have no doubt
that fanaticism is
dangerous. And of all
the books in the world
on life, I have no doubt
that the life of one
person weighs more
than them all.

<hr>

What is man?
Ally of God or
simply his toy?
His triumph or
his fall?

<hr>